GENDER IN FICTION

A COLLABORATIVE EXPLORATION

with:

MJ LaBeff, Michele Barrow-Belisle,
Bibiana Krall, Julia Satu,

Edward Selender, Caroline Harbour,
Jennifer C. Lopez and

Gordon A. Wilson

IS IT WORTH TALKING ABOUT?

Gordon A. Wilson

A simple question that led into a much bigger discussion. The conversations have educated me and raised more questions. My benign first question— "Are there blatant giveaways as to the gender of an author?" I think that's where it began, or at least what I was trying to ask. I know, it could run down the wrong road easily and that was not my intent— it was an innocent question. Let me use an example, a particular passage in a man/woman love scene mentioned the woman arching her back in a particular way. Something about the description made me feel it was written from a female perspective. Not that it matters, trust me here. It is nothing I could put my finger on, the scene was done very well. I can't go into the details of what made my thought train go down those tracks but it got me thinking.

There may be things I write which give away my gender as an author? I have to put a question mark on that because it is a question. Does it matter? I can't say if it does or not unless of course, it does—then it does and vice versa. Better question- does it make a difference? I think it could if I were unintentionally writing something insensitive for example. What if I have such a limited understanding of the psychology of the opposite sex that my female characters were totally unbelievable? There is a big, "What if?" that would make it matter and make a difference. What if the same were true of the male characters I write?

I have been a man the better part of my life, I like to think a manly man, whatever that means— and I tend to see things from my perspective. I can't say it is a particularly male perspective but someone else may. I don't have much to compare it to, as hard as I try to see anything from more than my personal perception. I would love to learn more on this subject. As authors we set out to explore some of the pertinent aspects of gender in writing. Please join the conversation for an opportunity to share ideas and learn.

PEOPLE SHARE COMMON NATURE...SO WHAT ABOUT GENDER?

SHE SAID, HE SAID

MJ LaBeff

From Genre Wars to Gender Wars in fiction writing… and to think this all came from a few #tweets that led to several email discussions! As one of the writers on the subject of choosing an appropriate genre for your work of fiction, I couldn't resist adding my two cents here. My first reaction about male versus female writers was this: women speak more words per day than men. Now, you're probably wondering, what does this have to do with writing fiction?

Not so many months ago I was listening to the radio and heard about a study conducted by Luanne Brizendine, a practicing physician at the University of California-San

Francisco and author of The Female Brain. Brizendine states women speak an average of 20,000 words a day versus 7,000 words for men. It struck me as interesting because being a female writer I'm cognizant of the way men speak to each other and to women. I can write "girl" but can I write "boy"? Ah, ha, now you see where I'm going with this. When I'm writing dialogue for a male character I have to think like a man. How would a man say it? If men only use 7,000 words a day, I have to write a male character's dialogue direct and to the point.

This is a good place to share a story. My husband and I are both busy people. Often times when he asks me a question I'll start to respond and he'll say, "Just answer the question" to which I reply, "You have to know

the backstory." He doesn't in reality.
Does this sound familiar? Being a gal
I feel safe to say that women tend to
be chattier than men. A friend of
mine says when he's ready to leave a
party he lets his wife know twenty
minutes earlier because that's how
long it takes her to say good-bye. I'm
sure you have similar stories to share,
and I hope you will. Through these
daily interactions we can learn and
improve upon writing male and
female characters.

"Can we talk man to man?" Ever
wonder where the expression came
from? Me too. According to the Free
Dictionary by Farlex "man-to-man" is
an adjective, marked by candid
interaction between men and
characterized by directness, candour,
openness; it is forthright and honest.
Farlex goes onto explain it is

straightforward in means or manner or behavior or language or action. I found it interesting the expression hasn't become shared universally to include women too. However, wouldn't it be odd if a female character approached another character and said, "We need to talk man-to-man"?

There a several fiction rules I remember learning when I started writing, fear not you can break rules- it's your book, your story, so write it as you may. However, some rules are important, I'll let you decide on this one: write like your audience is a bunch of sixth graders. I know it sounds insulting, considering I write suspense and thriller novels for adults, but it really means that most people read at a sixth grade level and in other words keep it simple so a reader doesn't have to pause and figure out who said what or reread a passage to understand where the story is going. This led my mind to wonder. Do men write better, more succinctly because of their direct and to the point nature, not to mention only speaking 7,000 words per day? I think not. You wanna know why? Ha-ha, I can't fool you. You got it. Male writers have to think like women too, assuming their stories have female characters.

Well there's my two cents for what it's worth.

WOMEN VERSUS MEN:

WRITING CHARACTERS OUTSIDE OF YOUR OWN SPHERE

Bibiana Krall

This question of gender is an interesting one. I have had more than one row about this topic with other writers.

I am in grad school, currently in my final semester for a Master's in Creative Writing. I am continuing in academia with my M.F.A and plan on teaching at the University level. This question will be a terrific topic to teach. The gender question is becoming more and more relevant, as the literary world is finally connecting to alternative voices.

As a woman, mother and a working novelist, I must understand what motivates one person over another in a story. I do not write of merely Caucasian middle class females, so there has to be respect first.

When I begin writing, it is imperative that I fairly navigate the emotional levels of my character. I do not think like a man; I think like a woman. So how do I get inside the head of someone unlike me?

I have a more straightforward approach. I first consider what they are up against. So I give them a socio economic landscape, then their culture, then their gender. I am a gourmet cook and I can tell you, the only way to make a fantastic key lime pie is to use the ingredients in a very specific tried and true methodology.

It is extremely important to speak, know or observe someone in this group you are portraying, unless of course we are talking about monsters, aliens etc. Then the sky is the limit. Yet, even monsters sometimes procreate, so the physical connections are important as well.

Getting inside the head of a male character is tough for me, but doable because I have three brothers who are all very different and a husband whom is willing to answer the weirdest possible questions. Writing about men is the toughest aspect about what I do. Sure I have had a few crazy-exes that would make fierce antagonists, but once in awhile, a good guy would be awfully nice in a story too.

Do I think a man can write under a pen name and fool us when he speaks as a teenage girl with severe anxiety or an elderly woman from Africa who watches rebels raid her village? I think a person can get awfully close, but it comes down to an understanding of motivation and how a conclusion is reached in this mindset, rather than the results.

If you look to Classical Literature, a female POV will normally offer more emotional content or inner monologue, while a male POV alternatively offers more action or body language. I see this played out in a constant weekend scenario at my own house.

"Hey honey, let's go see a movie."

"Sure babe, what's playing?"

"Trash, chick-flick, something where things get blown up..."

You already know how this is going to go right?

So, as a female... I would potentially surprise you, because I would probably pick the third. Never underestimate the power of choice, but be mindful of taking yourself out of the equation and really listening to what that particular character wants, needs and desires. Gender matters, but that is merely the beginning. At the end of all this, we are individuals. I would not propose to say if an emotion is male or female. It is merely part of the fabric of that particular person. Writer or character, male or female, in the long game these all can be moot, if you do your homework.

I read a book a few years ago written by a body language expert who spent 30 + years working for the FBI in interrogation. He had a lot to say about how much any human communicates with merely expression, eyes lowered etc.

We all communicate that way, but what an elderly male Italian fisherman would do versus a fifteen-year-old female Syrian refugee are night and day, looking at the same exact situation.

If you really want to go deep... let's talk about the most infamous and argued about study of body language by, Dr. Albert Mehrabian. (I am not sure if I agree totally with his findings either. But he was thinking about it, and took the time to form a more structured opinion.) 93% of communication considered as body language is awfully high. If men do not observe women, now stop right there!

I have a pretty good idea of where your brain just went. Ha ha! I am laughing because mine did too...

I mean... driving a car, on the phone, and laughing with friends. Then attempt to write about them in their voice. If you don't, it's going to be off big time. Same thing goes for the other side of this argument.

Albert Mehrabian (born 1939 to an Armenian family in Iran), currently Professor Emeritus of Psychology, UCLA, has become known best by his publications on the relative importance of verbal and nonverbal messages. His findings on inconsistent messages of feelings and attitudes have been misquoted and misinterpreted throughout human communication seminars worldwide, and have also become known as the 7%-38%-55% Rule, for the relative impact of words, tone of voice, and body language when speaking. Mehrabian also constructed a number of psychological measures including the Arousal Seeking Tendency Scale.[1] – Wikipedia

You are a writer...you probably already know all about this complexity. So, it's important to dial into your memory of situations and to utilize that knowledge, regardless of your gender and of whom you write.

Observation and a keen sense of what your aim is, that's integral. Would this person in real life actually think, talk, feel, or respond this way?

Of course there is always the Rough Rider. That one person who doesn't think, speak, act or do anything one might expect. That would be a fun person to write!

The bottom line is this…

If you are writing outside of the skin you have been given, do everything in your power to know their origins and what would truly be important to that person. If you take the time to get to know this about your character, they will come to life and ring true to your readers. The greatest challenge would be to have that person in our life read and offer drop dead, honest feedback.

I am chuckling about this question right now. A writer I casually know is attempting to write as a female in her early twenties going through a rough patch while also pregnant. He asked me to give my opinion, as to why it wasn't going well. I have not had a ton of interaction with him, but he isn't very dialed into me and more than likely not to this woman in his story either.

My advice to him was watch TV shows about women in that age group that accidentally got pregnant and to read, 'What to Expect When you are Expecting'. That book is the Holy Grail to all women when they are pregnant. I was gifted with four copies when I made my happy announcement.

He refused. Now he says, 'I just can't get her right'… I don't ever say, "I told you so"— but. Just don't expect to be able to write intelligently about it, if you don't care about the character's feelings, experiences and physical needs.

I have no intention of writing to any certain extent about the male POV. Why? Am I anti-male? A man basher? No, not at all. I am simply pro-female and one of my goals is to inspire women to connect with their inner goddess, to grab life and be stronger in their choices.

So, do I really think a man can write like a woman?

Yes. But he needs to do it carefully, respectfully and with a keen eye on motivation, before action or emotion are added to the mix. Every, single thing we do as humans has an emotional trigger beneath it. Incorporate that little gem, and darling— I think you've got a winner. Good luck with it!

GENDER WARS?

Edward Selender

When Gordon first asked me to join in on the topic of Genre Wars, I immediately thought of Gender Wars as well. Initially as a pun, then—like Gordon, it became a benign hunch that there might be some writing style differences between men and women, in their writing style. As Gordon correctly queries, perhaps it doesn't matter, unless the male or female writers make insensitive remarks, or write about the opposite gender with lack of understanding that leads to less-than-credible characters.

MJ also astutely questioned, how, if there were discernible differences, female writers, using a male nom de plume (classic British writer George Eliot and

British mystery writer, P.D. James immediately come to mind) could have fooled audiences into thinking they were male. Both excellent points.

As a former Psych major, I would preface my comments by saying, the fact that we know the author's real gender ahead of time (especially in the above examples of female authors we now know were writing under male names) could create something akin to a confirmation bias in which we inadvertently find evidence that conforms to our "hypothesis." So, for example, if we believe women display certain traits in their writing, we are more likely to find examples, in the writings of authors we know are female, and ignore examples which refute this belief.

One characteristic I notice, in many works by female writers, is the emphasis on clothing or fashion. This is displayed in

Suzanne Collins' Hunger Games, Collins emphasizes the attractive reaping day clothes worn by the girls, such as the pretty "expensive white dress" worn by the mayor's daughter Madge, as well as how her blonde hair is "done up with a pink ribbon". Additionally, protagonist Katniss Everdeen remarks how her mother has "laid out one of her own lovely dresses for me. A soft blue thing with matching shoes."

In Dead Ringer, there's a conversation between attorneys Bennie Rosato and Anne Murphy, which goes on for two pages, about pantyhose. Hard to imagine a male author writing this. Additionally, there's a conversation, among the female attorneys, about one of the young associate's dyed hair, in which Murphy raves "it's so cute! Lipstick pink! I love it."

Do the above examples matter? Not to me.

They certainly don't detract from the story (OK, the stuff about the pantyhose did seem to go on a bit long). In fact, I like the playful way Bennie pokes fun at her own looks with self deprecating humor.

On the other hand, if a male author had written in a derogatory way, about women's emphasis on clothing/fashion (I sincerely hope female writers will not think I am poking fun at women; I certainly am not)—this would be an issue. In Fifty Shades of Grey, EL James' character, Anastasia Steele starts off the first chapter complaining about a bad hair day. As in the previous examples, I pose the question, does this have an impact on the story?

Steele later makes a cryptic comment to herself, "Oh dear, is Blonde Number One in trouble?" after the third blonde secretary she encounters, in Christian

Grey's office, inquires if either of the previous secretaries had offered Anastasia anything to drink. One wonders if a male author would have written such a line.

In this case, Anastasia is remarking on the apparent superficiality of a man having three blonde female secretaries. This could be seen as worthy social commentary, a positive thing in my view, which DOES make a difference.

In Jane Austen's Emma— Emma Woodhouse's preoccupation with, and pride in, her matchmaking abilities, seem like more of a female attribute. Does this matter? Not in terms of the quality of writing here. Again, just an observation.

Although I have never read Fifty Shades of Grey all the way through, I did see the movie (it was a really cold day, around V-Day of course, the movie I wanted to see wasn't playing and, ahem... like all

Blockbusters, this was playing 50x that day- lol). Anyway, I was interested that Christian Grey was focused on sex and would not even allow Anastasia Steele to sleep in the same room with him initially. Whereas, towards the end of the movie— Grey responded to Anastasia's need for romance and she seemed to begin understanding Christian's world (kind of a Don Quixote- Sancho Panza kind of thing).

This may be a stereotype, but aren't women perceived as more romantic? I happen to be very romantic, myself—at times. I once compared a girl I had a crush on in high school to Queen Guinevere. It's often said however, that guys have only one thing on their mind. Again, as a Psych major, I tend not to believe in extremes (like nature—nurture), but maybe this is true, in general.

According to one article in the Atlantic,

female authors, such as Collins and Rowling dominate YA fiction and— according to Market Watch.com, men prefer to read non-fiction whereas women prefer to read fiction. Do those stats matter? Not necessarily, however, one other statistic I came across seemed problematic.

Per Quora.com, men are more likely to read books written by men, whereas women are more gender neutral in that regard. This could be perceived as a problem, or 'an area of opportunity'. One woman I recently discussed this with thought perhaps this difference may be caused by societal norms.

According to Paul Oswell (www.theguardian.com), a 2014 Goodreads survey found that "80% of a new female author's audience is likely to be female." Oswell also stated that JK Rowling's publisher, Bloomsbury decided to use her initials because "they thought young boys were less likely to read [her young adult books] under her full name".

A final interesting stat, which may support my thoughts on gender and romance came from a 2014 Nielsen Romance Buyer Survey, commissioned by Romance Writers of America. According to this study, women make up 84 percent of Romance book buyers, and those buyers tend to also read (key word "read"), in general, "Mystery, General Fiction, Cooking/Food books, Young Adult, and, yes… Erotic Fiction." Does that mean women don't read or write other genres? Of course not.

Unfortunately, I haven't read any books, yet, written by women using male pen names. However, I did read the beginnings of P.D. James' The Lighthouse and George

Eliot's, The Mill on The Floss. One thought on how these authors were able to fool their audiences is that they weren't writing in First Person Point of View.

For whatever it's worth, the above are just some of my thoughts on possible gender differences with regard to writing styles and reading preferences. There's actually much more to this than I had envisioned and would love to read other opinions on this.

GENDER, WRITING, AND EDUCATION

Caroline Harbour

When I was in Seventh grade, I read a book called, The Outsiders in school. It's a mainstay of many middle school English departments because it has a lot of substance, the writing is skillful without being stuffy, and middle-schoolers can relate to it. It's a story of a small brotherhood of teenage boys growing up as "Greasers" in the rough part of town and trying to navigate typical teen problems, along with the unique challenges that come with their status, or lack thereof.

The book is credited to S.E. Hinton, and when my seventh grade English class got through the last chapter and flipped to the author bio on the back cover, we were all shocked to find out that S.E. stood for Susan Eloise; the rough and tumble coming-of-age story with an almost entirely male cast— was written by a woman. Our teacher told us that the book's publisher was afraid young readers wouldn't believe a female author could convincingly write a story like this, so they used a gender neutral configuration of her name. When I got to high school we heard a similar speech about Mary Shelley's Frankenstein, and the fact that no one (at that time) believed a 19-year-old girl could have written this story as well as she did.

Conversely, in my college English department the overwhelming majority of the books we study were written by men, though the department itself is largely taught and populated by women. I was never a big fan of Austen or the Brontë sisters growing up, so the classics that I loved were almost all written by men. Even today, if you ask me to start ticking off some of my favorite authors, the list would look something like this: John Steinbeck, Orson Scott Card, Garth Stein, George Orwell, Barbara Kingsolver, C.S. Lewis, Dr. Seuss, E.B. White, Alexander Dumas, Marcus Zusak. Only one of my top ten is a woman. What does that say about my taste, the taste of readers in general, or the skill of female or male writers as a demographic?

I believe the stories we grow to love when we're young can have a profound impact on not only the kind of readers we turn out to be, but the kind of people we turn out to be. The characters we admire teach us what traits are commendable, what's worth fighting for or against, what relationships look like, what happy endings look like. Everyone has that treasured book or series from childhood or adolescence that spoke to exactly what you were feeling when you couldn't speak it yourself. As I said, my lack of fondness for Romantic or British Fiction growing up left me with limited options as far as female authors we would study in school were concerned.

But when I think of the stories I loved growing up, I don't just think of what we studied in school, I think of what I read on my own time. Zilpha Keatley Snyder's, The Egypt Game, the first chapter book I read on my own, my beloved Laura Ingalls Wilder box set, Eleanor Estes' delightfully quirky Pye family books, and Judy Blume's signature humor, which I read and loved just as much as Shel Silverstein's poetry and Jack Wilder's adventure novels.

What I'm getting at here is that great stories are great partly because they transcend the limitations of the genre or the audience they were written for. Good stories don't have to be for a particular demographic; I might even go so far as to say great stories cannot be confined to a particular demographic, because they tap into what it means to be human above all else which, is what allows so many people to connect with them. As Bibiana said, and rightly so, it takes research, empathy, and effort to write from a perspective that is very far removed from your own. Those are all qualities that the authors I've mentioned no doubt possessed in order to create what they have. And they used them just the way authors should, to make their readers invest in and care about their characters.

Does the gender of the author matter to a piece of writing? I think it would be naïve to say it doesn't. But to let what we know as gender, in all its culturally specific, whitewashed, boxed-in limitation, define who can write what— who can read which genres— or what books are "male" or "female", would be to miss out on a lot of great stories.

WRITING FROM WITHIN...

IDENTITY

Jennifer C. Lopez

All this writer's talk of gender perspective in literature reminded me of an incredibly thought-provoking article in Junctures: The Journal for Thematic Dialogue. It was the 'Epistolary Revelations of Five Writers,' in which they each share their personal interpretations on the experience of writing together collectively. The end result, a collaborative story. The authors spoke of their own individual commitment to the challenge of allowing themselves the deep feelings and experiences that would come of their own writing; as well as those of their peer collaborators, during the writing process.

What does this have to do with gender identity in writing?

The project required intimate authentic exchanges, in order to bring about a "community consciousness." The authors would prepare by talking about what their writing together might look like or feel like—how they would each be "seen" by their peer writers while writing back and forth, and so on. One stated, "We would pose questions so rich and unanswerable or present dilemmas so enticing that everyone would chime in with responses. Sometimes serious, sometimes silly, sometimes downright dire." Their individual points of view became beautifully woven together as one voice at times, despite dramatic differences of opinion or an alternative stance on a particular topic. How could something like this occur? The question could only be answered by going to the depths. The writers were willing to risk their own vulnerability for the sake of the project, for the sake of understanding one another and feeling compassion for their fellow writers' positions.

So that's why collaborative writing came to mind immediately for me, as something quite connected to the concept of gender differences in writing- as well. Before beginning any collaborative writing myself, I researched this topic in depth, wanting to understand the differences between writing collaboratively and writing cooperatively. The difference fascinated me, and how little there was on the subject! The one article I mention, was intriguing enough because it powerfully conveyed the natural evolution of each author's voice transforming from a group of individuals into one. The completion of one beautiful story was the collective effort all the authors, but a reader would have to look deeply to decipher an individual voice, if even possible.

Isn't it really all about personal identity—our talk of understanding how to adequately interpret and portray characters of a distinct gender from our own, in writing? I think it boils down to an ability to stretch the limits of our imagination as authors, striving to understand human vulnerabilities and behaviors more intimately— by feeling them ourselves. As writers, we can become immersed in a sense of compassion for our character's plight, even irate over what we have made them do. When we 'write our characters'— and their distinctive identities are richly portrayed—their role in the text becomes one readers can connect with —no matter the gender.

Deeply connecting with our characters' identities, we enter another world through their eyes. For the good or bad, we understand and feel what it's like to walk in that individual's shoes. We've quite literally, gained the first steps in our ability to recognize another perspective—one different from our own—and can begin to fully write from within it.

There are expressive and emotional males, while there are cold and frigid men. Likewise, there are tough as nails, cut-to-the-chase women, while there are gushy sensitive ladies. If we dig deeper, challenging ourselves to connect with our individual character's rationale and perspectives, the writing flows—along with the creation of an authentic character. Identifying with our character's personal moments, triumphs, failures, deepest thoughts and misfortunes help shape them fully within the story, whatever their gender. The character becomes significant to the reader when understood intellectually and emotionally by the writer.

Writing from the perspective of a gender other than our own, I can't help but think of my work as an interpreter. We must want to learn, study and understand the culture beneath the words and feelings in order to do them justice in the interpretation. We as authors, are interpreting and conveying others' human experiences (possibly distinct from our own) using the most accurate translations we can. These interpretations have their basis in our efforts to understand and connect with their meaning— from a distinct vantage point. It would be difficult for me not to draw this connection between interpreting the human experiences of our characters and a deep thoughtful translation; since that is a part of what I do as a Bilingual Interpreter. Genuine compassion for our characters has everything to do with our ability as writers to present them so that any man or woman will appreciate this illumined identity.

Translations, interpretations and

collaborative writing all seem to whole-heartedly support the point that a character of the opposite gender is born of making the connection that the voice of any good writing must be 'collective,' even if it's only derived from the 'confines' of our own mind. Ultimately, good writing must include our ability to think both as others and as one.

THAT'S WHAT (S)HE SAID.

AS QUOTED BY A MALE FRIEND WHO WAS READING MY WORK:

"UM, YEAH, GUYS DON'T SAY THAT SH*T"
Michele Barrow-Belisle

As a psychology-major, I've made it a habit to people-watch, (my *'excuse'* for being super-nosey, according to some) and I've always found the behavioral differences between the male and female gender quite fascinating. Add to that the time spent ~~eavesdropping~~ *studying* conversations for general writing purposes, and well, I supposed my observations might border on *stalkerish*. I've noticed so many interesting differences, yet they don't seem to stay within those clear-cut lines. Which makes sense given the fact that humans don't fit into nice neat easy to label packages. But setting aside the many-hued differences of our world, I would definitely say that yes, there are marked differences, sometimes overt, often very subtle, but small telltale signs that indicate the gender of the author. Often. Not always.

When I decided to write a novella for my teen book series, from a male character's POV, (Freeze) I did my research. A *lot* of research. Because I was aware of not only how my character's voice needed to stand apart from my teenage, female protagonists' voice, but also the fact that he was kind of a badass, alpha-male character, from an imaginary realm and race of Shadow Fey. Those differences alone made him difficult to write. He was a warrior and a knight, and the antihero... and while the Fey often have androgynous traits *physically*, his personality was all alpha. So what was a poor female author to do?

I did my homework. I paid close attention to books written in the male perspective by not only female authors, but also male authors. The differences were slight, but definitely noticeable, which means to a certain degree they were somewhat important in getting the character's voice right. I also used my husband and son as sounding boards when something didn't quite sound right. It was very helpful, and often hilarious, to get the male perspective in the flesh.

How important is it to get it right? Well, I suppose it's as important as getting *any* character's voice right. It just has to be believable, and the reader will just assume they're reading the male POV, no questions asked. I do recall instances where I've read passages that were supposed to be the male POV and they didn't sound believable for me. And because sometimes things like that are elusive and hard to put your finger on, I just did as much due diligence as I could, then listened to the male character's voice inside my head and wrote what he said.

DOES GENDER MATTER?

Julia Satu

Authors write differently for different genres. For example, authors who write young adult or romance novels, typically write for women, who are their predominant audience. These authors are also often women— maybe because "It is better to write about things you feel than about things you know..." (L.P. Hartley) These stories are about coming of age and carry an emotional theme. Readers here are looking to connect with the protagonist.

The gender of an author should not matter, but it does. I find this shifting slowly, but a bias is still present. This is evidenced by some female authors using initials instead of their first names. It is said that J.K. Rowling's publisher thought boys would be less likely to read Harry Potter and the Philosopher's Stone, if it was known that a woman wrote it.

How sad is that?

I'm sure a woman who writes great young adult or romance novels could also write a kick-ass thriller or adventure story. J.K. Rowling wrote a crime fiction novel under the pseudonym: Robert Galbraith, giving the 'author' a background in military and security. Would the book have been less likely to be published if the author were a woman? Would it be less believable? It sounds like her editor must have thought so. Once he found out who 'Robert Galbraith' really was, he said, "I never would

have thought a woman wrote this."
(Robert-galbraith.com)

I find this disappointing in two ways:
the editor's bias mirrors society's and
Rowling's own— since she was
delighted by the comment. Rowling
could have just as easily used a
female name with the same
background, but again, the novel may
have never been published.

What this example shows, is that
Rowling simply did her research (as
well as master writing in the
protagonist's voice). She didn't
actually need to morph into a man to
write a 'manly' book. Research is the
key. Research is required by every
writer and not just for historical
fiction.

Some authors may need to do
research on personality types or even

on the reactions of the opposite sex if they lack the knowledge, just like if they were to place their story in a setting or culture they were unfamiliar with. Last year, I saw this tweet from a fellow author: "So writing from the perspective of a woman is a lot harder than anticipated. Any advice? #amwriting #amwritingfantasy #writerslife" I responded, asking for specifics and his question was, "What is a girl thinking when she's talking to a guy she is interested in?" I found the whole concept of reaching out on social media for research about women fascinating and wrote a blog post about the exchange. This author did the right thing. He wasn't sure so he did his research. As writers get more experience and learn to observe the world around them with a keen and unbiased eye, they will become better writers. Writers need to immerse themselves in life, learn new cultures and research their topics thoroughly. If they don't, they run the risk of creating stereotypes within their stories.

The best advice I have for new authors is to have a diverse group of beta readers, who enjoy your genre and who will give you their honest opinion, no matter how painful it may be. It will only make you a better writer.

WRAPPING IT UP

I don't think I can add much after all of this, to improve it. It is safe to say- the subject is interesting. Each author presents a different way of looking at the subject and even where the opinions overlap it helps to read them from a unique perspective. Each contribution gives me at least one way to see from a perspective other than my own. I sincerely hope it does the same for you. Happy writing, reading and living. My sincere gratitude to all who have contributed to this fascinating, educational conversation. –Gordon A. Wilson

MORE ABOUT THE CONTRIBUTORS-

MJ LaBeff- Author: *-Mind Games, -Last Summer's Evil (The Last Cold Case series)*
https://mjlabeff.com/

Jennifer C. Lopez- Author:
-Thanks, But I'll Teach My Own Kid. The New Generation of Fearless Homeschooler, -A Beautiful Mind- The Spark of Introversion, -Fakebook. The Empathy Power Series
http://www.thejennieration.com/

Michele Barrow-Belisle- Bestseller: *-FIRE & ICE (Faerie Song Saga Trilogy)* www.MicheleBarrowBelisle.com

Julia Satu- https://juliasatu.com/

Caroline Harbour-
https://www.theodysseyonline.com/@carolineharbour

Bibiana Krall- Author: *Carolina Spirit, Escape into the Blue, Leaving Pandora*
https://www.bibianakrall.com/

Edward Selender-
https://writeaboutnowct.wordpress.com

Gordon A. Wilson- Bestseller: *Firetok* www.firetok.com

www.ingramcontent.com/pod-product-compliance
Lightning Source LLC
Chambersburg PA
CBHW050752290526
45792CB00008B/2152